And the Beat Goes On

And the Beat Goes On

KENNETH MULLER

ZOUEV PUBLISHING

Published 2015
Printed by Lightning Source

ISBN 978-0-9560873-5-5, paperback.

For Lynn Meredith Davidson Lemaire, educator extraordinaire, who always gave 200%... even when she probably should not have.

Thank you to Frank Masanta, Jr. for creating the Sun-spring Charity School and for including me in his wondrous works, to Frank and Margie Urie for their comic inspiration and support, to David Lavoie for his love of drama, to Santina Gambrill for her superb direction of the first production, to Marleen van Gyes for coming to all of my plays, to Neal Dilk and Alison Lipp for being compassionate, talented school administrators, to Brad Masoni for being a literary/musical genius and an asset of a colleague, to Gen Sparano for always being a beautiful role model - and to Alexander "Sasha" Zouev for inspiring me to publish.

Synopsis I:

And the Beat Goes On is a contemporary comedy, which examines the generational differences among children, parents and grandparents; these generational differences have always existed, but are they becoming more profound and potentially insurmountable as technology and social media become increasingly embedded in our regular routines and in our expectations of others? Under the aegis of a classic Greek chorus – well, maybe more comic than classic – the players experience the frustrations of keeping up with the new as well as with remaining connected with the old. Will the two continue to peacefully and productively coexist, or will they allow technology to drive an irrevocable wedge between them?

Synopsis II:

Teenagers, Oscar and Eva, struggle with the time constraints and parental/societal pressures that the present invariably imposes on the younger generation. Their parents, Grandparent and teacher have their own challenges – keeping up with technological advances, the culture of celebrity and... children on overload. The gang on Mount Olympus finds the developments disturbing and decide to intervene...or not.

Playwright and Sun-spring Charity School Information:

Playwright, Kenneth Muller, works as an international educator; he has taught English, history and drama around the world. During a teaching stint in Zambia, Kenneth did some volunteer work at the Sun-spring Charity School in Ngombe Township, Lusaka. The founder of the school, Frank Masanta, Jr., was jobless and begging on the streets just a few short years ago, and he could not afford school fees for his children, so he created a solution for them. Frank managed to get permission to use an abandoned building as a school for poor children. In addition to teaching his own children there, Frank welcomed (and continues to welcome) all children in the community who want to learn. At present, there are approximately one hundred students attending Sun-spring Charity School. Kenneth continues to work with Frank Masanta to improve the lives of children in Zambia; all proceeds from the sale of this script are earmarked for the children of Ngombe Township.

AND THE BEAT GOES ON

A Middle School Comedy (With Musical
Interludes) in Two Acts

by

Kenneth Muller

CAST: 14+ (a minimum of 5 females
and 5 males; Greek chorus members
can be of either gender)

Notes:

Musical selections were made based on simplicity of arrangements (one or two instruments) and appropriateness of theme, but the possibilities for substitutions are many. For example, the director of the first production in Rotterdam replaced "The Beat Goes On" with "Firework" (Katie Perry) as the closing musical number, and this worked well; the audience became energized and an enthusiastic curtain ensued.

As this production was written for performances at the American International School of Rotterdam, there are some local references; these can easily be adapted to the performance location. In addition, the script can easily be adapted as technology, text language and celebrities-in-the-news change by simply updating these.

Setting is flexible and sets are minimal; the songs selected require minimal arrangement and can also be substituted according to the director's vision/interpretation.

Cast of Characters

Greek Chorus Leader:

speaker with a powerful voice

Greek Chorus (3+):

the group can be as large or small
and will contain both genders

Prometheus:

The Greek God who brought fire to
mankind

Daedalus:

Father of the undisciplined Icarus

Eva:

A middle school girl

Joanne:

Eva's mother

Millie:

Eva's Grandmother

Kaitlyn:

Eva's school mate

<u>Oscar</u>:

A middle school student

<u>Myra</u>:

Oscar's very New York mother who
likes to mix Yiddish with English

<u>Irving</u>:
Oscar's father

<u>Mr. Jacobs</u>:

A history/social studies teacher

<u>Scene</u>

Anywhere

<u>Time</u>

The present

Scene 1

SETTING: Full stage

AT RISE: Cast members emerge from
                            both sides of the stage
                            and perform the song, "My
                            Generation," written by
                            Pete Townshend.

FULL CAST/ENSEMBLE

People try to put us d-down (Talkin' 'bout
my generation)
Just because we get around (Talkin' 'bout
my generation)
Things they do look awful c-c-cold (Talkin'
'bout my generation)
I hope I try after I get old (Talkin' 'bout
my generation)

This is my generation
This is my generation, baby

Why don't you all f-fade away (Talkin'
'bout my generation)
And don't try to dig what we all s-s-say
(Talkin' 'bout my generation)
I'm not trying to cause a big s-s-sensation
(Talkin' 'bout my generation)
I'm just talkin' 'bout my g-g-g-generation
(Talkin' 'bout my generation)

This is my generation
This is my generation, baby

Why don't you all f-fade away (Talkin'
'bout my generation)
And don't try to d-dig what we all s-s-say
(Talkin' 'bout my generation)
I'm not trying to cause a b-big s-s-
sensation (Talkin' 'bout my generation)
I'm just talkin' 'bout my g-g-generation
(Talkin' 'bout my generation)

This is my generation
This is my generation, baby

People try to put us d-down (Talkin' 'bout
my generation)
Just because we g-g-get around (Talkin'
'bout my generation)
Things they do look awful c-c-cold (Talkin'
'bout my generation)
Yeah, I hope I try after I get old (Talkin'
'bout my generation)

This is my generation
This is my generation, baby

(BLACKOUT)

(END OF SCENE)

2

ACT I

Scene 2

SETTING: Mount Olympus

AT RISE: GREEK CHORUS LEADER,
                      GREEK CHORUS and
                      Prometheus are positioned
                      on stage.

GREEK CHORUS LEADER

Woe unto the mortals - yet again - who
never cease to compound their mediocrity.
Fie! Far below Mount Olympus, compassion
and communication are far worse than ever.

GREEK CHORUS

Even with all of their portable devices?

GREEK CHORUS LEADER

Trust me, they're not helping. Victims of
oblivious self-indulgence, both mortal
youths and elders alike do no longer
comprehend one another. On the fated day
that Prometheus dared to create the flawed
mortals from mere mud, Zeus did rightly
rise up in fury.

(emphatically)

Forsooth!

GREEK CHORUS

3

Bless you.

(GREEK CHORUS LEADER looks at chorus and
                rolls eyes)

                GREEK CHORUS LEADER

What have you to say for yourself,
                Prometheus? Speak.

                PROMETHEUS

I, Prometheus, creator of mortals and
carrier of fire, make no excuses. My
creation of the mortals was indeed a vane
and vein - yes both spellings - attempt to
replicate the perfection of us, the gods of
Olympus.

                GREEK CHORUS

An attempt which failed miserably.

                PROMETHEUS

Mighty Zeus would concur, but I stand by my
creations. Flawed as they are, some have
attained greatness and fostered the
compassion and communication of which you
speak: Albert Einstein, Madame Curie,
Nelson Mandela, Christiane Amanpour - even
Mark Zuckerberg.

                GREEK CHORUS

Thank you for not including "Oprah," but
what about the other seven and a half
billion mortals?

PROMETHEUS

True. They are not as productive as they once were, and many have become mired in reality television and senselessly addicted to constant and inane messaging. They've all but put Hermes out of work, but are they really all that bad?

GREEK CHORUS LEADER

Behold, Prometheus, the fruit of your misguided labours!

(BLACKOUT)

(END OF SCENE)

SETTING: In a kitchen

AT RISE: MILLIE and JOANNE are
                  working on a cooking
                  project; EVA looks on.

                    EVA

Blackberries are on sale this week. Can I
get one, Mom?

                  MILLIE

Don't be silly dear. Buy a whole case of
them, and I will make you one of my prize-
winning desserts. Myra Goldberg has been
trying to get the recipe out of me for
years. The secret is in the pastry.
First, you have to be sure to…..

                  JOANNE

Mother, let me handle this. Eva is talking
about a different kind of blackberry.

                  MILLIE

Nonsense. Last month it was a different
kind of apple and now a different kind of
blackberry? I'm not daft yet, dear.
Everybody knows that there are different
apples, but there is only one kind of
blackberry. I'm an old woman, Joanne - I
know my fruit.

                              EVA

No, Gran. A Blackberry is a phone - kinda
like an iPhone but cheaper.

                             MILLIE

iPhone!? The regular old ear phone is bad
enough. I guess the nose phone will be
next. I tell you, it's getting to be
ridiculous.

                             JOANNE

Beside, Eva, Blackberries are finished,
which is why they're on sale.

                             MILLIE

So blackberries are finished.
(shakes head)

Always something new to make life more
confusing, but I do my best to try to keep
up with it all, you know. Didn't I buy you
that Jessie Baxter CD just last year?

                        EVA AND JOANNE

Justin Bieber!

                             MILLIE

And didn't I take you all out to the mall
last month to treat you to the latest
frozen concoctions at Star Trek for your
birthday?

                        EVA AND JOANNE

Starbucks!

                    MILLIE

I even spent hours with you watching Miles
Davis do that new twerking thing on all of
the news shows.

                EVA AND JOANNE

Miley Cyrus!

                    MILLIE

I thought he looked different.

                    JOANNE

You're right, Mom - you have been trying.
We all appreciate the efforts you make.
Unlike you, young lady. A little more
conversation time with your Grandmother
wouldn't kill you.

                    EVA

But it's SOOO boring. I have to repeat
everything like three times, and Gran still
gets it wrong.

                    JOANNE

Then make it five times. And without that
Blackberry to suck up even more of your
time, you'll be able to spend a little more
one-on-one with her.

                    EVA

That is totally unfair. Thanks a lot,
                    Gran.

                    MILLIE

Joanne, please don't punish Eva because of
me. I'll just have to try harder. They
say the crossword puzzles help keep the
brain sharp, but I guess they're not
working.

                    JOANNE

It's hardly a punishment - she already has
too many devices. Just last week, she got
the PS4.

                    MILLIE

Oh, dear. That sounds serious? Is there a
treatment for it? That could explain why
she doesn't speak very much.

                    JOANNE

You got that right, Mom.

                     EVA

See what I mean?!

                    JOANNE

Yes, I see what you mean, but I also see
what your Gran means. It is high time for
you to spend less time gaming and more time
"Granning."

                          EVA

What's in it for me?

                        JOANNE

I'll tell you what's in it for you –
getting to know and appreciate family. Try
to think a little bit beyond yourself.
Besides, you are a good teacher when you
want to be. If it weren't for you, I'd be
lost - LOL, BFF, OMG, OCD, USB. Life was
much simpler when it was just TGIF and MTV,
but if you have a teenage daughter, you
have no choice but to learn this stuff, so
I do.

                        MILLIE

I remember having done the same for you
back in the day. Let me tell you - learning
all of the hippie language was a challenge.
And an embarrassing one at that.

                          EVA

If you did it before, you can do it again,
Gran. Instead of baking cakes all day and
doing crossword puzzles, you could learn to
game and Tweet, Instagram and Facetime.
You'd be a newb
[short for "newbie," a newcomer to an
online game] for a while, and take a lot of
crap from other players, but…

                        JOANNE

Eva! Don't be so rude to your Grandmother.
I'm sure she's not interested in all of
that game nonsense.

                    EVA

Then it's her own fault that she's clueless
and can't keep up. The world didn't stop
in 1980.

                  JOANNE

No, it didn't, but good music sure did.
There sure are a lot of sad excuses for
talent these days… like that band you used
to like. The one that just broke up. New
Directions. That's it.

              EVA AND MILLIE

One Direction!

                  JOANNE

Oops.

                  MILLIE

That's not entirely true, Eva. I had to
learn all sorts of new technologies when I
was young too. Trust me – the first
dishwashers were no picnic and learning to
hook up a VCR was more complicated than
building a spaceship, but
I managed.

                    EVA

What's a VCR?

                    11

JOANNE

Enough, Eva! And what about you? Don't
you have to make some kind of effort too?
I thought we raised you to be caring,
considerate, patient.

EVA

Yeah, but... old people are too much work
sometimes. They always want to talk and do
stuff together. Who has time for that?
And it is so not fun.
(EVA looks at her phone)
New game starts in five minutes. G2G.
(exit)

MILLIE

What on earth is G2G?

JOANNE

I wish it meant "Go to Gran."

MILLIE

I'm sorry, dear. I didn't mean to cause a
scene. You and Brad have been so good to
me, and I really do try my best with Eva.
Perhaps she's right - I'm just an old,
useless relic, past my sell-by date. When
people mention
apples and blackberries, I just want to go
and bake a pie.

JOANNE

Don't listen to her, Mom. You're doing
fine. It's her job as a Granddaughter to
adjust to your ways, right? To adapt? Be
flexible? We've all had to do it, right?

                    MILLIE

New outfit, dear? Is that really what
they're wearing these days?

(JOANNE looks at the audience.)

                 (BLACKOUT)

               (END OF SCENE)

SETTING: The living room of MYRA
                            and IRVING

AT RISE: IRVING and MYRA and their
                            son, IRVING are in their
                            living room; IRVING is
                            sitting and reading the
                            newspaper; MYRA is
                            standing over him.

                        MYRA

Irving, he's driving me meshugge. Get your
toches upstairs and tell Oscar to put the
iPad down and pick up a book.

                        IRVING

(reading a newspaper)
Yes, dear.

                        MYRA

How is this possible, I ask you!? Our son,
the schlemiel who's failing social studies.
He comes from a family of historians! What
did I do to deserve this?

                        IRVING

Don't know, dear.

                        MYRA

Such a shande. Imagine what the neighbors
must think.

                    IRVING

Yes, dear.

                    MYRA

The chairman of the PTA and my son is
failing history. Talk about embarrassing?!
I'll never get re-elected if that nudnik
doesn't get his act together. If that
happens, I'll make his life miserable, and
I'll have plenty of extra time on my hands
to do so. Are you listening to me?

                    IRVING

No, dear.

                    MYRA

Excuse me?!

                    IRVING

I mean, yes, dear.

                    MYRA

You think this is funny? You think this is
                    normal?

                    IRVING

Maybe it's just a phase he's going through,
dear. We've all…

                    MYRA

Oh no you don't. Not that **it's-just-a-phase** thing again. Why does everybody in your family think crazy behavior is just a phase? Your sister is fifty, and she still talks to the microwave oven, and your father still fixes everything with duct tape.   Phase shmaze! This is your family's fault – there's no lifeguard on duty at that gene pool. My mother tried to warn me, bless her.

(enter OSCAR, face in iPad. He walks past his parents not noticing them. His face never leaves the screen of his device.)
Hello to you too, Oscar.

                    OSCAR

Sorry. I was just checking PowerSchool to see if the grades for the history quiz are posted yet. Here it… (hesitates) …uh, I guess the teacher didn't get around to it yet.

                    MYRA

Let me see that thing. You failed another one didn't you?

                    OSCAR

Just a little bit.

                    MYRA

That's it. Your father and I are not going to have a son who knows bubkes about history, are we Irving?

                    IRVING

Yes, dear. Uh, no, dear.

                    OSCAR

Lighten up, will you, Ma? It's only one
class. I'm doing fine in important classes
like science and math, so you should be
happy. Besides, history is useless. Who
cares what happened way back when? It's
the future that counts.

                    MYRA

Are you listening to this, Irving? (no
reaction from IRVING)
If there were no history, Oscar, there
would not be a future - or a present for
that matter. Do I have to remind you how
much your grandparents suffered during the
war?

                    OSCAR

They lived in Miami during the war.

                    MYRA

The humidity down there is a killer. And
all of those insects. Oy vey! And the
tourists!

                    OSCAR

Good try, but that has nothing to do with
history.

                    MYRA

                    17

Don't be such a wisenheimer, Oscar. We
study history so that we learn from our
mistakes and don't repeat them.

                    OSCAR

Really? Then why are the two Koreas still
at it? Care to explain Syria? Sudan?
Afghanistan?
                    MYRA

Alright already. I get it. You're keeping
up with current events on your iPad - fine-
but it would be nice to see you with your
social studies books once in a while?

                    OSCAR

(waving his iPad)
Hello?! Wikipedia?

                    MYRA

Wikipedia, huh?! Well, we are sickapedia
of this nonchalant attitude toward
education. Either the failures in social
studies become history or that iPad does.
Right, Irving?

(no response from IRVING)

Irving? Irving, what's that in your ear?

                    OSCAR

Dad! That's my iPod. I've been looking
for it all week.

                    IRVING

Trust me, son. I need it more than you do.
(MYRA gives IRVING a whack.)

(BLACKOUT)

(END OF SCENE)

ACT I

Scene 5

SETTING: Back on Mt. Olympus

AT RISE: DAEDALUS and the GREEK
                    CHORUS are conversing.

DAEDALUS

I, Daedalus, did unwittingly plunge into
the abyss of failure as a father. Having
permitted the arrogance of my son, Icarus,
to swell and fester unrestrained, the
dearest of prices I did pay. My cursed
apathy in the art of parenthood did leave
me sonless. In my defense, how could the
idiot actually believe he could fly to the
sun?

GREEK CHORUS

Kids think they know everything. Mortal
children are no different.

DAEDALUS

Mortal children of today do know more.
They must. They study our foibles and
failures at school in order to learn from
them. No need have they of oracles and
soothsayers, for they have Macbooks and
Internet.

GREEK CHORUS

And pretty soon, Google glasses.

20

DAEDALUS

They have survived the Reagan and Bush
years. Witnessed natural disasters,
inequities, financial and societal crises.
Surely the wisdom and knowledge of today's
mortals comes close to surpassing ours.

GREEK CHORUS

A nice theory. But they worship
Kardashians, make wealthy celebrities of
criminals. They still think Adam Sandler is
funny, and let Dennis Rodman be an
ambassador to North Korea? Is this wisdom?

DAEDALUS

Your point is taken. Confer shall I with
Hera, wife of Zeus, goddess of marriage and
family. The mortals must close the rift
between young and old, techie and non
techie - either willingly or by Olympian
meddling. For eons, refrained have we from
intervening in earthly madness, but it
might be time for a long overdue visit.

GREEK CHORUS

Proceed with caution, Daedalus.
Interfering with fate can have treacherous
results. Forget not the tragedy of
Oedipus.

DAEDALUS

Alas, poor Oedipus, in earnest attempt to
prevent the prophesy from coming to pass,

21

did unwittingly kill his father and marry his mother.

GREEK CHORUS

Talk about a dysfunctional family. And we're worried about the mortals?!

DAEDALUS

Focus not on our blunders but on our feats. True, there was Pandora's Box and Medusa, but we created the forests, the seas, the mortals and the whole of the solar system, including the sun without which none of these could thrive.

(DAEDALUS and the GREEK CHORUS are joined by the rest of the cast. The whole ensemble will perform "Always Look on the Bright Side of Life" by Eric Idle and John du Prez.)

FULL CAST

Some things in life are bad
They can really make you mad
Other things just make you swear and curse.
When you're chewing on life's gristle
Don't grumble, give a whistle
And this'll help things turn out for the best...

And...always look on the bright side of life...
Always look on the light side of life...
If life seems jolly rotten
There's something you've forgotten
And that's to laugh and smile and dance and sing.

When you're feeling in the dumps
Don't be silly chumps
Just purse your lips and whistle - that's
the thing.

And...always look on the bright side of
life...
Always look on the light side of life...

For life is quite absurd
And death's the final word
You must always face the curtain with a
bow.
Forget about your sin - give the audience a
grin
Enjoy it - it's your last chance anyhow.

So always look on the bright side of death
Just before you draw your terminal breath

Life can give you stress
And mortals are a mess
Life's a laugh and death's a joke, it's
true.
You'll see it's all a show
Keep 'em laughing as you go
Just remember that the last laugh is on
you.

And always look on the bright side of
life...
Always look on the right side of life...
(Come on guys, cheer up!)
Always look on the bright side of life...
Always look on the bright side of life...
(Worse things happen at sea, you know.)
Always look on the bright side of life...

(I mean - what have you got to lose?)
(You know, you come from nothing - you're
going back to nothing.
What have you lost? Nothing!)
Always look on the right side of life...

(BLACKOUT)

(END OF SCENE)

SETTING: OSCAR and his social
studies   teacher, Mr.
JACOBS, are in   school
classroom.

AT RISE: OSCAR and MR. JACOBS are
                            sitting at a table with a
                            stack of books.

                    MR. JACOBS

Look, Oscar, I'm not real thrilled about
these tutoring sessions either, but your
grades are so far below C-level, that you
might want to think about a career in
submarines. Bah-dum-bam!

                      OSCAR

Hilarious, Mr. Jacobs. You might NOT want
to think of a career as a comedian.

                    MR. JACOBS

That's the thing – I might have to. School
inspectors are coming around next week to
evaluate the success of our programs, and
you're making us look bad.

                      OSCAR

And what does that have to do with you
becoming a comedian?

                    MR. JACOBS

My contract is up for renewal at the end of
the year and things are not looking great.
Might lose my job.

                    OSCAR

But why? You're a nice guy and the kids
all like you. It's not your fault social
studies class is so boring.

                  MR. JACOBS

It seems that it's all about this.
(he holds up his laptop)
The school district has decided to go
bookless, and everything will be done
online. I can send e-mails, check Facebook
and do your basic search, but I think these
guys are expecting a lot more than that.

                    OSCAR

Glad to hear about the bookless thing; the
textbooks we have are useless. I've tried
to read them, but end up on Facebook within
minutes. They just don't work for me.

                  MR. JACOBS

I admit that they are dire, but they're all
we have. Budgets have been tight the last
couple of years, and history doesn't really
change, does it?

                    OSCAR

But your lectures are okay - just too long.

                     26

MR. JACOBS

Could have something to do with your
attention span… just sayin'.

OSCAR

Fair enough. But what's your problem with
the Mac?

MR. JACOBS

Are you kidding?! Way too much new
terminology for me.
And I just can't seem to remember all of
the shortcuts.

OSCAR

Kinda like me with social studies.

MR. JACOBS

Point taken. It's not just the terminology
and shortcuts. Every time I try to do
something I think I know how to do, a
stupid box pops up asking me to synchronize
something, update an app, save something in
a cloud, or register something. I just
click "cancel", because I don't want to
screw everything up. Frustrating.

OSCAR

It's not that bad once you get the hang of
it.

MR. JACOBS

Not that bad?! It's overwhelming. Virtual desktops, a bunch of new passwords to remember, and what's this OSX that won't leave me in peace?

OSCAR

I think it's something like Microsoft is for PCs. It just makes other stuff work.

MR. JACOBS

And what was wrong with the mouse that had left and right clicks? That two and three-finger swiping nonsense just makes my documents vanish, never to return.

OSCAR

They're still there. You just have to swipe them back. No big deal.

MR. JACOBS

Maybe not for you. Anyway, enough about me and my problems. We're here to deal with yours.

OSCAR

Yours are more interesting – and easier to deal with.

MR. JACOBS

You really think so?

OSCAR

I know so, but you're right. Why are my
scores in your class so bad?

                    MR. JACOBS

You never really answer the questions.
Your answers are like the overly
complicated definitions on Wikipedia that
never really get to the point.

                    OSCAR

I study from Wikipedia.

                    MR. JACOBS

And you think the textbooks are bad? How
do you even understand that stuff?

                    OSCAR

I don't really, but I figure they must know
what they are talking about. And I am much
more comfortable studying from my computer
than from a dusty, old book with really bad
graphics.

                    MR. JACOBS

Basically, I think the Wikipedia people do
know what they are talking about, but it's
like they have robots putting all of the
information together. And talk about bad
graphics.

                    OSCAR

At least it's on a screen.

                    MR. JACOBS

29

Okay, I get it. Why don't we look at some different sites - ones that might actually help you?

OSCAR

That could work. Maybe we could help each other during these torture sessions?

MR. JACOBS

What do you have in mind?

OSCAR

I'm pretty much a Mac expert, and I can help you to learn some of the shortcuts and lingo.

MR. JACOBS

And in return, I hook you up with some social studies websites that are actually useful?

OSCAR

Or I just help you learn how to work this thing so you can keep your job, and I'll deal with the boring stuff later when I am in the mood.

MR. JACOBS

That's good for me, but it's not going to get your grades up and satisfy my bosses or the visiting inspectors. Not to mention your parents.

                    OSCAR

It was worth a try.

                  MR. JACOBS

And certainly tempting for me, but it
wouldn't be right, you know?

                    OSCAR

Yeah, I know. Listen, Mr. Jacobs, have you
ever thought about taking a different
approach in class?

                  MR. JACOBS

I've been doing the same thing for twenty
years, Oscar. I have my routines, my
notes, my hilarious jokes. How was the
Roman Empire cut in half?

                    OSCAR

(droll eye roll)
With a pair of Caesars.

                  MR. JACOBS
I love that one.

                    OSCAR

Why does history repeat itself?

                  MR. JACOBS

Because students don't listen the first
time.
(laughs and points to OSCAR)

                    OSCAR

Okay - we done with that?

                    MR. JACOBS

Right.

                    OSCAR

If you want to become less of a computer
dinosaur and you want your students to
become more interested and successful...
which would reflect on you...

                    MR. JACOBS

Go on. I'm listening.

                    OSCAR

Why don't you assign gaming time for
homework?

                    MR. JACOBS

Isn't that the same as not giving homework?

                    OSCAR

Not exactly. You would just be more in
control of the activities kids do to avoid
doing homework.

                    MR. JACOBS

And that helps...how?

                    OSCAR

Duh? History games.

                    MR. JACOBS
Go on.

                    OSCAR

Well, when we study Europe and the Second
World War, for example, you could assign
teams to play Call of Duty II,
Company of Heroes, The Saboteur – and there
are lots of others. The settings,
characters and dates are all real, and kids
will pay closer attention to that than they
will to a cheesy PowerPoint presentation or
a lame book.

                    MR. JACOBS

Well, I'd have to look at the games first
to see if they are indeed appropriate.

                    OSCAR

Let's play one now. Here, let me set it
up.
        (OSCAR reaches for MR. JACOBS'
laptop)

                    MR. JACOBS

No! Stop! Talk me through it and tell me
what keys to hit. If you do it, you just
hit a bunch of keys at lightning speed to
make things work, and I learn nothing. Too
much pressure.

                    OSCAR

Fair enough. First, go to Finder…

(BLACKOUT)

(END OF SCENE

ACT I

Scene 7

SETTING: Anywhere. A mall bench,
                     perhaps.

AT RISE: EVA and her friend,
                     KAITLYN sit across from
                     each other with phones in
                     hand. After the initial
                     "Hellos," the vocals of
                     this scene will be pre-
                     recorded   and played as
                     the girls text; the words
                     they text will be spoken
                     on the recordings. The
                     words the girls text will
                     be heard by the audience
                     via the recording; the
                     actors will not speak to
                     each other directly. The
                     girls have a conversation
                     via texts - even though
                     they are almost next to
                     each other.

                         EVA
                     (live)
Hi.

                     KAITLYN

                     (live)

Hi Eva.

                     (The girls begin texting
                     now. Their recorded
                     conversation - deliberate
                     and in texting pace - is

                          35

played in sync with their
respective texting.)

                    EVA

OMG. So glad to be out of the house. Mom
and Gran are being difficult again.

                  KAITLYN

Now what?

                    EVA

Can't get the new Blackberry, because I
have to babysit Gran.

                  KAITLYN

That's messed up. Why?

                    EVA

Mom thinks I have a problem communicating
with people. Is that a joke or what?

                  KAITLYN

Totally. What does she want you do?

                    EVA

Crosswords and boring conversations with
Gran about stuff I don't get. Something
Mom calls "quality time."

                  KAITLYN

WTH?

                    36

                         EVA

Right?!

                       KAITLYN

What you gonna do?

                         EVA

Ignore it for now. Just tell them I have
extra volleyball practices.

                       KAITLYN

But that's true. You do.

                         EVA

Oh right.

                       KAITLYN

But afterward, you can come to mine. We
can make cookies
for the team bake sale. BTW, can't wait to
raise the
money for the new uniforms.

                         EVA

Me too, but me, bake? LOL

                       KAITLYN

We have to. Coach said everything has to
be home-made or we're off the team.

                         EVA

No prob. I order them online and they are
delivered next day. They're home-made only
in someone else's home. I do it every
year.

                    KAITLYN

Really? I guess that's okay. I kinda like
doing it myself. My Mom is really into it,
and I get to lick all of the bowls. You
should try it some time.

                    EVA

I did once, but my Gran noticed, and it
turned into months of torture.

                    KAITLYN

OMG - What did she do?

                    EVA

She got all excited and my Mom made me sit
and watch two seasons of the Great British
Bake Off with her.

                    KAITLYN

I kind of like that show - except for the
old lady who
finds fault with everything.

                    EVA

I know. "Soggy bottoms. Soggy bottoms."
Give it a rest.

                    KAITLYN

Maybe you could give it a go when your Gran isn't around?

                    EVA

She hasn't left the house since 1995, and the kitchen is her territory. If I go in there, she makes me wash something, eat something or make something - with her. Too much hassle. Too much pressure.

                    KAITLYN

I guess that doesn't sound like too much fun.

                    EVA

Ya think?! I mean, I love her and all, but what a time vampire.

                    KAITLYN

Okay, Eva - G2G. Time for practice.

                    EVA

Me too.

(The girls put their phones away and get up to leave together. They speak live to one another on their way off stage.)

                    KAITLYN

I hope the locker room doesn't smell like feet and cheese today.

                    EVA

Has it ever smelled like anything else?

(BLACKOUT)

(END OF SCENE)

ACT I

Scene 8

SETTING: Full stage. No set.

AT RISE: Cast emerges from all
                    side of the stage and
                    sing/dance to "Under
                    Pressure" by David Bowie.

FULL CAST/EMSEMBLE

Pressure pushing down on me
Pressing down on you no man ask for
Under pressure
That burns a building down
Splits a family in two
Puts people on streets

Bah bah bah bah bah bah

It's the terror of knowing
What this world is about
Watching some good friends
Screaming let me out!
Pray tomorrow takes me higher
Pressure on people
People on streets

Do do do bah bah bah bah
O-kay
Chippin' around
Kick my brains round the floor
These are the days
It never rains but it pours

People on streets
People on streets

It's the terror of knowing
What this world is about
Watching some good friends
Screaming let me out!
Pray tomorrow takes me higher higher higher

FULL CAST/ENSEMBLE (Cont.)

Pressure on people
People on streets

Turned away from it all
Like a blind man
Sat on a fence but it don't work
Keep coming up with love
But it's so slashed and torn
Why why why?
Love love love love

Insanity laughs under pressure we're
cracking
Can't we give ourselves one more chance?
Why can't we give love that one more
chance?
Why can't we give love give love give love?
Give love give love give love give love
give love?
Cause love's such an old fashioned word
And love dares you to care
For people on the edge of the night
And love dares you to change our way
Of caring about ourselves
This is our last dance
This is our last dance
This is ourselves under pressure
Under pressure
Pressure

42

(Sound of thunder crashing)

MILLIE

(to the audience)
That was exhausting. I think it's time for
an interruption.

FULL CAST

Intermission!

(BLACKOUT)

(END OF SCENE AND ACT I)

INTERMISSION/INTERVAL

ACT II

Scene 1

SETTING: In JOANNE'S kitchen

AT RISE: JOANNE, MYRA, MILLE,
                  IRVING and MR. JACOBS are
                  having coffee and
                        cake around the
                  table. IRVING   is a
                  bit detached, reading the
                  newspaper while the
                  others converse.

JOANNE

I can't tell you how lucky I feel to have
good neighbors like you , and it's so nice
to be able to get together once in a while
for a coffee.

MYRA

And for some of your mother's outstanding
baking. I feel like I could platz, but I'm
still gonna have another piece.

MILLIE

Why thank you, dear. That means so much
coming from a connoisseur like you. I know
that your parents came from the old world,
so they must have brought you up on the
real stuff.

MYRA

They sure did. My mother's schnecken and
noodle kugel were to die for!

44

MILLIE

I knew it! A few years back, I took the
Luftwaffe back to the old country...

(Myra shots a horrified look)

JOANNE

She means Lufthansa - sorry.

MILLIE

Yes, that's the one. Don't get me wrong.
The museums were marvelous, and the quaint
towns were like something out of a
storybook, but the bakeries! After eating
those treasures, there's no way I could buy
things here, so I do it all myself.

MYRA

If only I had the time... and the recipes,
Millie. Hint, hint.

MILLIE

Of course. It's just that I haven't
written them down yet. Never seem to get
around to it.

MYRA

Well, I admire the value you place on
tradition, Millie. If only the rest of the
family did. Mishpokheh - but what can you
do?! You can't choose them.

JOANNE

I think I know exactly what you mean. And you have no
idea how helpful it is to have a friend and neighbor
who's also coping with a difficult teenager.

                    MYRA

Misery loves company, right? My husband
isn't much better.

(to IRVING)
Irving, be a mensch and put down that
newspaper! It's called social skills?
Good manners?

(to guests)
And he wonders why Oscar always has his
face in some device. Have you ever seen
such a role model?

                    IRVING

(putting away his paper)
FYI - that's exactly what I'm trying to do...
model proper reading for the boy.

                    MYRA

And how's that working out for you?!

(to the guests)
That's why Mr. Jacobs is here today. He's
been tutoring Oscar, and I thought it would
be a pity for him to miss out on Millie's
baking.

                    JOANNE

Mr. Jacobs is always welcome here. He's
one of Eva's favorite teachers.

MR. JACOBS

Thank you, and please call me Eric. I must
tell you that your baking gets my highest
scores.

MILLIE

Even back in the day, I have to admit that
the Russian judges would never score me
lower than a five on my baking. He wasn't
so kind with some of our Olympic figure
skaters and hockey players, but whatever.

JOANNE

Let it go, mother.

(to MR. JACOBS)
And how is the tutoring going, Mr. Jac…,
                    Eric?

MR. JACOBS

So far, it's been very successful indeed.
We just keep ripping through those apps.
And I…uh…we… have learned lots of cool
shortcuts.

MYRA

That sounds promising, I think. Shortcuts
are always helpful. Fingers crossed for
the big exam tomorrow.

IRVING

47

(looking up – finally – from his newspaper)
Mind if I ask your expert opinion, Eric?

                    MYRA

Oh, it speaks.

                 MR. JACOBS

Not at all, sir – shoot.

                    IRVING

Why on earth would a school decide to go
bookless when the kids never even open
them?

                 MR. JACOBS

With all due respect, Irving – may I call
you Irving? – I think you answered your own
question. If students don't use them, why
waste money on them?

                    IRVING

Let me get this straight. You're a
teacher, and you think books are a waste of
money?

                 MR. JACOBS

I never said that. I grew up in the book
era – not that it's over yet…I hope, and I
read them all the time. And please don't
think this transition is an easy one for
me. I'm not as young as I look.

                    JOANNE

48

But do you agree with the no-book decision,
Eric?

                    MR. JACOBS

Not entirely, but that's only because I'm
old school. I think a combination of books
and online resources would be the best
solution, but maybe not the most realistic.

                      MYRA

And why wouldn't that be realistic?

                    MR. JACOBS

Okay. Just last year, my department bought
a whole set of history texts for a high
school group. You know what the kids did?

                     MILLIE

I'm afraid to guess.

                      MYRA

I think Wikipedia is in on this. It's a
big money-making
conspiracy.

                    MR. JACOBS

(continues to address IRVING's question)
They found the text online, downloaded it
and left the books in their lockers for the
entire year. When they returned them, they
were all in mint condition, and trust me –
that has never happened before.

MILLIE

But they still read the books, that loaded
version, right?

MR. JACOBS

Most of them did, and that's also never
happened before, which is awesome. Get out
the scales and judge for yourselves…what's
worse?

IRVING

Call me a relic…

MYRA

You're a relic. Trust me.

IRVING

(continuing as if he had not been
interrupted)
…but I don't think it's right. My son,
Oscar, already spends enough of his time
with his face in screens. It's not
healthy, I'm telling you.

MR. JACOBS

How much time is enough or too much? I
can't really answer that. Depends on the
kid, really… and the parents.

JOANNE

Sounds like that makes us – all of us – the
guinea-pig parent generation.

MR. JACOBS

I'm afraid it does. This situation is a
new one for the
world, and we have to find a way to make it
work to everyone's advantage.

IRVING

Sounds like too much responsibility to me.

MILLIE

Parenting has always been a behemoth of a
responsibility. Before computers there was
the disco era and the sixties. Hardly a
picnic for me.

JOANNE

I'm sorry, Mr.... Eric, but I have to agree
with Irving. Eva does the same thing, and I
really feel that all of that virtual
socializing is keeping her in-person social
skills from developing.

MILLIE

I'm her Grandmother and she hardly ever
talks to her me, and I do try to be
interesting. This stays here in the room,
but every once in a while, I buy one of
those teen magazines, so I can keep up with
antics of Jackson
Thunderbolt and Kathy Parnell.

JOANNE

(aside to the others)

Justin Timberlake and Katy Perry.

(IRVING and MR. JACOBS nod in recognition)

                    MILLIE

But it doesn't seem to do much good. She's
always plugged in, or - and this sounds
terrible to say - bored with real life.

                  MR. JACOBS

Oooh. This is a tough one. I don't mean
to sound like a teacher or like I'm passing
judgment, but it is up to the parents to
try to create the balance that works best
for all involved.

                    MYRA

I just want to rip those devices off of
Oscar and throw
them in the bin.

                   JOANNE

And sometimes I think that if I don't do
the same to Eva, she'll never get to know
her grandmother. That would just break my
heart.

                  MR. JACOBS

Would that really solve the problem or just
create a new one?

                   IRVING

What's that supposed to mean?

MR. JACOBS

You want Oscar and Eva to have friends,
don't you?

IRVING, MILLIE AND MYRA

Of course we do.

MR. JACOBS

If you took away all of their devices as a
punishment or as a way to try to make
things the way you want them to be, you
would simply be cutting them off from their
peers. That would be a disaster. I mean,
they are both only children; that would
just make them… "only-er."

MILLIE

That doesn't sound too good.

MR. JACOBS

It's not. Kids teach each other an awful
lot, and I see it every day. They are in
this new multi-device, cyberspace world
together, and they need to help each other
through it.

JOANNE

Fair enough, Eric. But what about that
healthy balance? I get the friends thing,
but what about family?

MR. JACOBS

Wasn't it always kind of like that, Joanne?
Think about when you were Eva's age. Did
you really want to spend that much time
with your parents?

                    JOANNE

Well, since my mother is here, I can't
really answer that, but I get your point.

                  MR. JACOBS

There's another very important issue here.

                    IRVING

What's that?

                  MR. JACOBS

Without good IT skills and a knowledge of
how all of the devices work, kids - well,
not just kids - are at a serious
disadvantage when it comes to getting and
keeping a good job.

                    MYRA

So true. Even at Starbuck's. Just to make
a cup of coffee, you have to be able to
push all kinds of buttons and codes. I
couldn't do it.

                   MILLIE

We went there once with Eva. I just love
Star Trek; they always write my name on the
cup so I won't lose it.

                     54

JOANNE

Or maybe so you won't forget your name.

(Millie gives an affirmative nod to her
JOANNE)

IRVING

It's true, Eric. Every once in a while, I
check out the classified ads in my paper.
The "skills required" sections are written
in some kind of secret code. And what on
earth is a Transparency Enhancement
Specialist?

MILLIE

A window washer maybe?

IRVING

Oy - the work farce!

MR. JACOBS

I do believe that all of you are making my
point for me.

JOANNE

I think we are. Thanks for counseling
session, Eric. The only question now is:
Where do we go from here?

(BLACKOUT)

(END OF SCENE)

55

SETTING: Full stage.

AT RISE: Cast is in place and
                            sings/performs "Teach
                            Your Children Well" by
                            Crosby, Stills, Nash and
                            Young

FULL CAST/ENSEMBLE

You who are on the road
Must have a code that you can live by
And so become yourself
Because the past is just a good bye.

Teach your children well,
Their father's hell did slowly go by,
And feed them on your dreams
The one they picked, the one you'll know
by.

Don't you ever ask them why, if they told
you, you would cry,
So just look at them and sigh and know they
love you.

And you, of tender years,
Can't know the fears that your elders grew
by,
And so please help them with your youth,
They seek the truth before they can die.

Counter Melody To Above Verse:
Can you hear and do you care and
Can't you see we must be free to

Teach your children what you believe in.
Make a world that we can live in.

Teach your parents well,
Their children's hell will slowly go by,
And feed them on your dreams
The one they picked, the one you'll know
by.

Don't you ever ask them why, if they told
you, you would cry,
So just look at them and sigh and know they
love you.

(BLACKOUT)

(END OF SCENE)

ACT II

Scene 3

SETTING: Mount Olympus

AT RISE: GREEK CHORUS LEADER and
                      GREEK   CHORUS are
                      positioned for an
                      important meeting.

GREEK CHORUS LEADER

By Zeus, some of the mortal parents appear
to be making a most valiant effort to
reconcile some of the chaos down there.
Prometheus would be pleased with this
change of course.

GREEK CHORUS

Parents, yes. Would that the offspring
would follow suit.

GREEK CHORUS LEADER

Ay, children continue to be the most
formidable of challenges. Even the mighty
Zeus, with all his wisdom, keeps his
current children at Olympic Day Care.

GREEK CHORUS

All three hundred and twenty-four of them?

GREEK CHORUS LEADER

Patience was never his strong point; forget
not that he did swallow his first five

children - Poseidon, Hades... and the other
three.

GREEK CHORUS

Talk about strict parenting?!

GREEK CHORUS LEADER

There is no other way. A firm hand is
required.
Otherwise, they are too easily lured into
the realm of making really dumb choices.

GREEK CHORUS

Like Pokemon or Grand Theft Auto.
Sometimes even a 'Lil Wayne songs on their
playlists.

GREEK CHORUS LEADER

As dangerous as we all know curiosity to
be, I have decided to succumb to it. Bring
me the children! I wish to hear what they
have to say for themselves.

(enter OSCAR and EVA)

GREEK CHORUS LEADER

Oscar and Eva, you have been summoned here
in the name of almighty Zeus to explain
yourselves.

EVA

Is this a dream?

GREEK CHORUS

Kind of.

                    OSCAR

Cool. Very *Clash of the Titans*.

              GREEK CHORUS LEADER

If you mean the latest one with good
special effects, then yes.

                     EVA

What do you mean "explain ourselves?" We
don't even know you. Besides, we aren't
supposed to talk to strangers.

                    OSCAR

Especially ones dressed like… well, in
stuff like that.

(points to the GREEK CHORUS LEADER)

              GREEK CHORUS LEADER

Insolence! Release the Kraken!
(a pause)
Just kidding – only Zeus can do that.

                 GREEK CHORUS

It's a good line though.

              GREEK CHORUS LEADER

Since, as you say, this is just a dream, no
harm can come to you, so do indulge me.

                    OSCAR

Fair enough.   What do you want to know?

               GREEK CHORUS LEADER

You mortals lead very strange and complex
lives. This cannot be denied. Over the
centuries, we have seen many changes - some
for the better, some for the worse.

                     EVA

Yeah, that's pretty much what happens on
Earth. What's the big deal?

               GREEK CHORUS LEADER

The big deal, young lady, is that our souls
weep for the lost wisdom of our greatest
communicators - Socrates, Aristotle, Plato.

                  GREEK CHORUS

Even Sophocles and his plays. They DID
inspire
Tarantino.

               GREEK CHORUS LEADER

(to GREEK CHORUS)
Silence!

(to EVA AND OSCAR)
Our philosophers ventured to your earth to
teach mortals
the value of communication, community and
family.

                    OSCAR

                     61

Did my parents put you up to this?

They would have if they could have.

GREEK CHORUS LEADER

We merely wish to understand why you
communicate so excessively with your peers...
albeit indirectly most of the time, yet
leave your family members to wallow in
frustrating isolation.

GREEK CHORUS

We're not too happy about the social
studies grades
either, Oscar. Our story is in that
curriculum!

EVA

(to OSCAR)
Yep, our parents definitely set this up...
unless this is a dream.

(pauses to think)
If that's the case, we must have guilty
consciences.

OSCAR

Yeah, right. Like we're both having the
same dream. That doesn't happen.

EVA

Look, Mr. Greek God...

                    GREEK CHORUS LEADER

Not yet, but thank you.

                          EVA

(continues)
You and your friends here have been around
for-like-ever. You seem to have nothing but
time.

                     GREEK CHORUS

True. We just won't die.

                         OSCAR

And, unless I'm missing something, there's
not a whole lot of high-tech stuff going on
up here.

                          EVA

No electronic devices and social networks.

                 GREEK CHORUS LEADER

We don't need them, for we can simply
appear where and when we wish.

                          EVA

Lucky you. We don't have that luxury.
There are a lot of expectations down there
- family, friends, school, society.

                         OSCAR

And that 24-hour day you guys created is
just way too short. If I'm not mistaken,

it's your man, Helios, who drags the sun
around us on his chariot. Do us a favor,
and tell him to slow it down.

GREEK CHORUS LEADER

I'm impressed. Your tutorial sessions are
paying off. Still, it seems like your
families are your last priority.

GREEK CHORUS

Shouldn't they be your first?

OSCAR

That's rich coming from you guys. Zeus
overthrew and banished his father, and
Achilles abandoned his. And if
Zeus were on earth, he'd be arrested by
social services for - well, for several
things - but keeping your son tied to a
rock for eternity as a punishment? Come
on.

GREEK CHORUS LEADER

Continue, mortals. You have my ear.

EVA

I can assure you that I love my Mom and
Gran, and I would never do anything like
that to them.

OSCAR

My parents are really irritating, but I
know they mean well. And I do love them.

GREEK CHORUS LEADER

If this be the truth, why then do you spend
more time gaming and texting with friends
than you do satisfying their parental
needs.

OSCAR

I'm not sure, but it sounds really bad when
you put it like that.

EVA

I guess I know that mom and gran will
always be there for me, no matter what I
do.

GREEK CHORUS

And your friends are not quite as
forgiving?

EVA

Exactly right. Kids can be brutal. Once
you lose your social reputation, it's
almost impossible to get it back. But
family isn't like that.

GREEK CHORUS LEADER

Seems like your peers have much in common
with Zeus.

OSCAR

I don't think they're as mean as he is, but
sometimes it feels like they come close
enough.

EVA

There are times when I am impatient with
Gran. She starts to sing this old song,
"You Always Hurt the One You Love." Then,
she just chuckles and gets on with things.
She's pretty cool, actually.

OSCAR

And my Mom screams her head off all the
time. Sometimes I think she does it just
to have an excuse to go off in
Yiddish, and sometimes I think she's just
frustrated with dad and taking it out on
me.

GREEK CHORUS LEADER

Enough about what they do! We are here to
discuss what YOU do. Do you honestly
believe that you do your part to make them
feel needed and successful as parents?

OSCAR

You're talking about the bad grades again,
aren't you?

GREEK CHORUS

A bit of a nag, isn't he? He too is a
father.

GREEK CHORUS LEADER

And as such, I expect subservience and
obedience from my children.

EVA

We don't really do the subservience thing down there anymore, but Oscar and I are pretty much obedient.

GREEK CHORUS LEADER

But is obedience enough?

OSCAR

I'm assuming that's a rhetorical question.

GREEK CHORUS LEADER

You've had your say, and your wisdom, though limited, is not as flawed as we had expected it to be. We have made our decision.

(Loud crash of thunder)

(BLACKOUT)

(END OF SCENE)

SETTING: Bare stage

AT RISE: EVA and OSCAR are
                  standing together, alone.

                    OSCAR

Okay, that was weird.

                     EVA

What was weird?

                    OSCAR

Getting told off by those Greek dudes.

                     EVA

I was hoping that was just my imagination.

                    OSCAR

No, no. It happened, but I'm not sure what
it was all about.

                     EVA

I think they made it pretty clear.

                    OSCAR

But why us? We're only kids - and not the
bad ones.

                     EVA

If those guys really want to fix things
down here, I can think of better places to
start. Africa could sure use them.

                    OSCAR

Or maybe even in their own backyards. I'm
no business genius, but how many times does
Greece need to be bailed out before it gets
its act together?

                    EVA

True. That place has been a mess for a
while now ... the last hundred year or so
if my history is correct.

                    OSCAR

Whatever. It's still a huge problem.

                    EVA

But maybe it's not the kind of problem the
gods - or whatever they are - get involved
with.

                    OSCAR

So they prefer bullying kids?

                    EVA

Come on, Oscar. That wasn't bullying.
We've both seen enough of the real thing to
know the difference.

                    OSCAR

Fair enough. But what makes my bad grades
at school more important than malaria in
Africa or the Greek economy?

                    EVA

My grades are fine, but they had a go at me
too.

                    OSCAR

Yeah, because you're not BFFs with your
Grandmother. How weird is that?

                    EVA

I don't think they expect me to be her BFF,
but I know I could be a little nicer to
her. They were right about that. And you
aren't exactly son of the year.

                    OSCAR

Okay. But we were right too. There just
isn't enough time to do all of the things
that everyone expects from us.

                    EVA

I know. It's way stressful, but maybe we
do spend too much time on the useless stuff
and not enough time on the more important
stuff.

                    OSCAR

My parents give me that "priorities"
lecture all the time, and I really don't
need to hear it again.

                              EVA

Clearly it is something we need to think
about.

                             OSCAR

No time for that right now; I have a
schoolwork emergency.

                              EVA

Me too. I have to get my cookies ordered.

                             OSCAR

How can cookies be a schoolwork emergency?
Unless, of course, you use them to bribe
teachers.

                              EVA

Long story. My volleyball team is having a
bake sale tomorrow to raise money for new
uniforms. The coach is an eco-, bio-freak,
so everything has to be homemade and
organic.

                             OSCAR

And that's an emergency?

                              EVA

For me it is, because whoever doesn't
deliver the good is off the team.

                             OSCAR

Strict coach.

                    EVA

Tell me about it.

                    OSCAR

Good luck in the kitchen then.

                    EVA

Me in the kitchen? Not happening.

                    OSCAR

So the cookies are going to bake
themselves? Or maybe you can get the
Greeks to send a batch down on a lightning
bolt.

                    EVA

Close. There's a lady somewhere around
here who takes online orders for organic
cakes and things. If I order them in the
next hour, they'll be delivered at school
tomorrow by morning break. It's awesome; I
do it all the time.

 (EVA takes out her phone and begins to
place the cookie order)

                    OSCAR

That is awesome. Gotta love the Internet.

                    EVA

Great. I can't get a connection.

(OSCAR takes out his phone and does the same)

                    OSCAR

Let me try.

(pause)
Nothing.

                         EVA

Are you with Verizon?

                    OSCAR

No, MTN.

                         EVA

They can't both be out.

                    OSCAR

I'm getting a creepy feeling about this.

                         EVA

Creepy is not the word. If I don't show up
with those cookies tomorrow, organic psycho
coach will bench me for the rest of the
season.

                    OSCAR

I've got a bigger problem.

                         EVA

I don't think so.

                    OSCAR

Tomorrow is the last social studies test of
the semester, and if I blow it, I might
have to repeat the year and my parents will
kill me. Actually, my mother's nagging and
kvetching would be much worse than death.

                    EVA

I don't get it. What does that have to do
with not getting a connection?

                    OSCAR

Duh? Wikipedia?

                    EVA

Just use the textbook.

                    OSCAR

Right. As if that thing ever left my
locker.

                    EVA

You're kidding! I could never…

                    OSCAR

Please don't turn into my mother. Having
the Greeks in my face was bad enough.

                    EVA

Sorry.

                         OSCAR

And my tutor, Mr. Jacobs, isn't available
for help tonight. I'm finished.

                          EVA

Let's not panic yet. The Wi-Fi at home is
never out. My mom needs it for her work,
so we have super service. But
I'm going to have to hurry if I want to
place that order
in time.

                         OSCAR

Nice for you. Well, I did download a few
documents I guess I could read over until
service is back. Not the best way to go,
but a C beats an F, right?

                          EVA

You'll do fine. Sorry, but I gotta run.
Good luck, Oscar. See you later.

                         OSCAR

Sure..cool…, but… uh…Eva?

                          EVA

What is it?

                         OSCAR

About those Greeks. Maybe we ought to just
keep that between us. I mean…

                           75

                          EVA

What Greeks?

                         OSCAR

Exactly.

                          EVA

If we told people that we visited a Greek
chorus and got told off by them, we'd be
banished to the nerd section of the
cafeteria forever.

                      (BLACKOUT)

                    (END OF SCENE)

SETTING: Two separate scenes on
                          opposite sides of the
                          stage. On stage right is
                          JOANNE's kitchen, and
                                  on stage left is
                          the kitchen of IRVING,
                          OSCAR and MYRA.

AT RISE: On stage right, EVA is
                          working with MILLIE as
                          her mother, JOANNE, looks
                          on. On stage left, OSCAR
                          is at a table with his
                          parents. The action will
                          alternate (from stage
                          right to stage left,
                          beginning with the scene
                          on stage right).

                          JOANNE

Luckily, I'm ahead of schedule with work.
Otherwise, this wireless malfunction would
be disastrous. I can't imagine what
happened, but nobody in the neighborhood
has connected.

                          MILLIE

Maybe it just needs new batteries, dear.

                          JOANNE

No mother. It doesn't work like that.

                    MILLIE

Maybe if you just jiggle that box with the
lights on it. Always worked with my old
radio.

                    JOANNE

It doesn't work like that these days, Mom.

                    MILLIE

Just trying to help, dear.

                    JOANNE

I know. It's not a big deal… the Jurassic
techniques do work with toilet malfunction…
sometimes, and God knows, we've been
grateful for your tips more than once.

                    MILLIE

Well, I think it's wonderful. I never
thought I'd get to spend so much time in
the kitchen with my lovely granddaughter.

                    EVA

Actually, gran, I had no idea how much fun
baking with you could be. We made these
amazing cookies all by ourselves. I feel
like an artist.

                    JOANNE

This is a scene I have been wanting to
witness for a very long time. Gods of

                    78

cyberspace, thank you for taking a long
overdue nap!

                    EVA

(looking upward and smiling)

Yeah, thanks. Really!

(scene freezes and switches to OSCAR, MYRA
and IRVING)

                    MYRA

All I can say is we're so thrilled that you
came to us for help. We're not as useless
as you thought, are we?

                    OSCAR

I never said you guys were useless - just
annoying.

                    MYRA

Since when is a parent not annoying? It's
our job, bubele.

                    OSCAR

But do you have to be so good at it?!

                    MYRA

I never thought I'd be saying this, but I
am happy that you didn't schlepp that
social studies book of yours home. Working
together for common goals is what a family
should be doing. Would you look at us?!

                              IRVING

Don't get all schmaltzy yet, Myra. There's
still a lot of work to be done here.

(to OSCAR)
You seem to be okay with the Greek stuff
and with World War II - not sure how that
happened, and I'm not complaining - but you
are still shaky on Dutch history.
                              MYRA

I am just loving this!

(to OSCAR)
Okay, Oscar, if William of Orange was born
in Germany and ruled a part of southern
France, how did he end up speaking Dutch?

                              OSCAR

Because his father was also an annoying
parent.

                              IRVING

Correct. Some details maybe would help?

                              OSCAR

Right. When he was eleven, his father told
him that he would inherit a huge kingdom,
including the south of France.

            (a pause)

                              MYRA

True, Oscar, but you didn't answer the
question. If you do that on tomorrow's

test, I'm going to suffer from spilkes for weeks. Pay attention to the question!

                    OSCAR

What was the question again?

                    IRVING

Dutch! Why did William of Orange speak Dutch.

                    OSCAR

Right. His dad blackmailed him. William couldn't get his inheritance unless he was educated in the Netherlands, so he went to go to school in Breda.

                    MYRA

Perfect!

                    OSCAR

Don't worry. The questions will be in front of me on the test tomorrow, and I am pretty visual. Learning stuff this way is helpful but way harder.

                    IRVING

That's why books are so important.

                    OSCAR

Don't start again. I get it. But how do you two remember all of this stuff?

                    IRVING

I read the papers everyday, and history is
always repeating itself.

                    OSCAR

Yeah. I remember that conversation.

                    MYRA

And I was just born brilliant. Good genes…
from my mother's side, of course.

(enter MR. JACOBS)

                 MR. JACOBS

Hi, Everyone. Hope I'm not disturbing.

                    MYRA

Not at all, Mr. Jacobs. Is everything
okay?

                 MR. JACOBS

More than okay. The school inspectors came
today. The interrogation was so intense; I
almost expected the water board to come
out.

                   IRVING

Schools will never change.

                    OSCAR

And how did it go?

                 MR. JACOBS

Thanks to you, Oscar, I was able to tell them the difference between a UFO and a URL. Not only did I not lose my job - I got a promotion. You're looking at the district's consultant for the online social studies curriculum.

                    MYRA

Congratulations, Eric!

                    IRVING

Well done, Jacobs!

                    OSCAR

Cool. Did the online gaming info help?

                 MR. JACOBS

Didn't hurt, Oscar. Didn't hurt at all. Anyway, I see what you guys are up to - some pretty important stuff. Just wanted to share the good news… and wish Oscar lots of luck for tomorrow.

(to OSCAR)
Always go back to the questions, Oscar, and make sure you answer them… because you can.

                    MYRA

Is there an echo in here, or what?!

(scene freezes. Back to MILLIE, JOANNE and EVA)

                              EVA

Gran, you never baked gluten-free organic
cookies in your life, and these are
perfect.

                            MILLIE

The next batch will be even better now that
I know how rice flour works.

                              EVA

Without the Internet, I couldn't get a
recipe for coach friendly cookies, but you
managed anyway. You're amazing. How did
you know they had to be gluten-free?

                            MILLIE

I'm not blind yet, dear. Your coach just
has that look. Anyway, it's nothing, dear.
I've been baking since the
1940s, and I've loved every minute of it.
There was a time there, just toward the end
of the war, when I even had to make my own
flour.

                            JOANNE

And I complain about having to go to the
store. Guess we're pretty spoiled these
days, aren't we.

                            MILLIE

Nonsense, Joanne. You work full-time, you
take care of me and you've been both mother
and father to Eva since Joe died. You're
far from spoiled.

                               84

JOANNE

Thanks, Mom.

MILLIE

We all have different jobs to do at
different times of our lives. We just have
to make sure that we recognize what that
job is.

EVA

(Having listened to the preceding
conversation, EVA has become a bit
contemplative.)

I'm not so sure I've been doing mine.

JOANNE

Ah, but you are now, Eva. And now is what
counts.

MILLIE

Indeed it is. And now that I've made my
first batch of Organic, gluten-free
goodies, I want to experiment further. Eva
has promised me that once the Interweb gets
itself recharged, we are going to goggle…

EVA and JOANNE

Google.

MILLIE

85

Yes, we're going to Google up some new
recipes and try them out together. It's
high time I expanded my repertoire in the
kitchen.

                    EVA

And that baking assistant's job is still
open, right?

(freeze. Back to MYRA, IRVING and OSCAR)

                   IRVING

I think we're good here, son.

                   OSCAR

You know what? I think we are too. Not
only am I going to pass that test; I'm
pretty sure I'm going to ace it.

                    MYRA

Don't get too cocky. You'll jinx yourself.

                   OSCAR

Okay. Fingers crossed. Is that better?

                    MYRA

Eh.

                   OSCAR

You know, I wouldn't really mind doing this
more
often. I mean, if you like it too.

                              MYRA

Like it?! We LOVE it. Don't we, Irving?

                             IRVING

Well, I can't say I'd rather be mowing the
lawn. Let's see how it goes.

(thinking)
If this does become a habit, maybe we could
just cancel the Internet subscription and
save a few shekels. We only use it to pay
bills anyway. Imagine. We pay a big bill
to one company so we can use it to pay
bills to ten other companies. What a world
this has become, I tell ya.

                             OSCAR

Let's not get too crazy, dad. I do use the
Internet for homework and projects. And
don't forget about PowerSchool.

                       IRVING AND MYRA

All right, all right, already. The
Internet can stay.

                             OSCAR

Oy! That was a close one.

(freeze. Back to JOANNE, MILLIE and EVA)

                            MILLIE

So, am I going to have to use all of these
new acronyms if I start to use the
cyberweb?

                    EVA

No, no. Not at all. They're just
shortcuts people use for texting.

                    MILLIE

Oh, right. That's s relief. I hate that
texting crap, but the acronyms are kind of
fun, though, and using them makes me feel
ever so modern.

                    JOANNE

What are you talking about, mother?

                    MILLIE

Oh, Eva's just been teaching me some of the
new lingo. WTF - I'm gonna be late.

                    JOANNE

What?! Eva?! She's your Grandmother?!

                    EVA
(to JOANNE)
Chill, Mom. I taught her the older
people's version. WTF - where's the
funeral.

                    MILLIE

My BFF - I'll be right there!

                    EVA

                     88

(To JOANNE)
Best friend fell.

                    MILLIE

OMG - call an ambulance!

                    EVA

(to JOANNE)
Old man groaning.

                    MILLIE

BTW - I'm over here!

                    EVA
(to JOANNE)
Bring the wheelchair.

                    MILLIE

How fun is this, Joanne?! Ha!

                    JOANNE

Maybe generational bonding was not my best
idea. Did I open up another Pandora's Box!
Yikes!

                (BLACKOUT)

                (END OF SCENE)

ACT II

Scene 6

SETTING: Mount Olympus

AT RISE: GREEK CHORUS LEADER and
                      GREEK   CHORUS
                      are assembled on stage.

GREEK CHORUS LEADER

All's well that ends well.

GREEK CHORUS

That's from Shakespeare. Plagiarism is
stealing!

GREEK CHORUS LEADER

(rolls eyes, annoyed)
I know him. He won't mind. More
importantly, Eva gained
a greater appreciation for the things her
grandmother has
to offer, and Oscar admires his parents for
the knowledge
he did not know they possessed.

GREEK CHORUS

But did he pass the test?

GREEK CHORUS LEADER

Excessively. Furthermore, the oldies were
given an opportunity to reciprocate.

                    GREEK CHORUS

Tell us more.

                GREEK CHORUS LEADER

Oscar's parents helped him pass the exam,
Oscar helped Mr. Jacobs to keep his job,
and Millie pulled off the organic, gluten-
free cookie challenge to keep Eva on the
volleyball team. So despite our
misgivings, they managed.

                    GREEK CHORUS

So the mortals get another chance?

                GREEK CHORUS LEADER

Yes. It would appear that our intervention
has yielded great success for the mortals.
Zeus will clearly be appeased.

                    GREEK CHORUS

Intervention? What intervention?

                GREEK CHORUS LEADER

Did I not leave a message with you to give
to Hermes to deliver to Zeus?

                    GREEK CHORUS

Indeed you did, but Hermes is out sick this
week. Return to sender.

                        91

(a GREEK CHORUS MEMBER extends a rolled paper to the GREEK CHORUS LEADER)

(GREEK CHORUS LEADER gives a reflective pause)

GREEK CHORUS LEADER

Then it was not Zeus's lightning bolt which struck the network towers of the mortals?

GREEK CHORUS

Nope. Just a freak storm. Climate change... or whatever they are calling it down there these days.

GREEK CHORUS LEADER

Then fate has taken its course yet again without our interference. This is very good news. Old teach young, and young teach old. T'was ever thus, and so it shall ever remain.

GREEK CHORUS

The end...almost

(BLACKOUT)

(END OF SCENE)

ACT II

Scene 7

SETTING: Full stage

AT RISE: Full cast sings and
                      dances to "The Beat Goes
                      On" by Sonny Bono
                              (or, alternatively,
                      Firework" by Katy Perry…
                      or whatever cast and
                      director find suitable))

FULL CAST/ENSEMBLE

The beat goes on, the beat goes on
Constant change keeps messin' with our
brains
La de da de de, la de da de da

Old school rules were once the rage, uh huh
History has turned the page, uh huh
Online gaming is the current thing, uh huh
Rappers and hip-hop are the new kings, uh
huh

Chorus

The Internet's the place to shop, uh huh
We click and click and click and never
stop, uh huh
And men still keep on marching off to war,
uh huh
Even though nobody knows the score, uh huh

Chorus

Grandmas want to share and reminisce

93

Kids just want the class to be dismissed
Technology getting faster all the time
And Greek Gods still remind us of our
crimes.

Chorus

(BLACKOUT)

THE END

CPSIA information can be obtained at www.ICGtesting.com
Printed in the USA
BVOW05s0429240615

405751BV00001BB/5/P